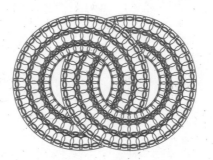

Dialect of
Distant Harbors

Dialect of Distant Harbors

Dipika Mukherjee

CAVANKERRY
PRESS

CavanKerry Press Ltd.
Fort Lee, New Jersey
www.cavankerrypress.org

Publisher's Cataloging-In-Publication Data
(Prepared by The Donohue Group, Inc.)
Names: Mukherjee, Dipika, 1965- author.
Title: Dialect of distant harbors / Dipika Mukherjee.
Description: First edition. | Fort Lee, New Jersey : CavanKerry Press, 2022.
Identifiers: ISBN 9781933880938
Subjects: LCSH: Belonging (Social psychology)—Poetry. | Kinship—Poetry. | Diseases—Poetry. | Families—Poetry. | LCGFT: Poetry.
Classification: LCC PR9499.4.M83 D53 2022 | DDC 821.92—dc23

Cover artwork: Gladys Simpson
Cover and interior text design by Ryan Scheife, Mayfly Design
First Edition 2022, Printed in the United States of America

 Made possible by funds from the
New Jersey State Council on the Arts, a partner
agency of the National Endowment for the Arts.

CavanKerry Press is grateful for the support it receives
from the New Jersey State Council on the Arts.
In addition, CavanKerry Press gratefully acknowledges generous
emergency support received during the COVID-19 pandemic
from the following funders:

The Academy of American Poets

Community of Literary Magazines and Presses

The Mellon Foundation

National Book Foundation

New Jersey Arts and Culture Recovery Fund

New Jersey Council for the Humanities

New Jersey Economic Development Authority

Northern New Jersey Community Foundation

The Poetry Foundation

US Small Business Administration

Also by Dipika Mukherjee

The Palimpsest of Exile (2009)

Rules of Desire (2015)

The Third Glass of Wine (2015)

Ode to Broken Things (2016)
   [Originally published as Thunder Demons (2011)]

Shambala Junction (2016)

This book is dedicated to my father, Kalidas Mukherjee, who didn't pass away from covid, but suffered from a Delhi-in-pandemic hell.

He taught me to love words and honor literature . . .
Papa, this is for you.

Contents

Wanderlust Ghazal

My language is a Bedouin thief, delighting in foreign sands;
It understands the erasure of monks, the ritual of
    palimpsests.

English has no word for Hemanta. No, not Autumn, nor
    Winter.
No Harvest Goddess in a veil of mists opaquely drawn.

The evening lamp in her hand gleams lambent through the
    fog;
Her voice merges into the howling wind. With abundance,
    desolation.

Every year, Mount Kinabalu is still wreathed in monsoon
    clouds.
Cloud messengers may be different, but some still speak of
    love.

Malay lascars sang of narrow boats, with pineapples
    stacked too high;
A grievous vastness to this world, beyond human
    experience.

Wanderlust is a disease. Incurable. Deep from within, it
    chortles,
The light of the moon cannot be rooted, Dipika, do not
    even try!

Bangkok, 1956

I will not be born for another nine years.

It is my father's first foreign posting; my mother is his bride. She leaves a sprawling home in Calcutta and fifteen play-mates to take his hand, crossing black seas to go where he will go. In a house as vast as her natal home there is the two of them, a maid, a gardener's family . . . only silence speaks her language through cavernous days.

He has not learnt to woo her. They both married when told.

But one day he brings home a sari from the Parsi merchant. *Look,* he says, unfurling a shimmer of cloth on their bed. *The rose color reminded me of you.*

He is color-blind.

She sees a snot-green of silk—it reminds her of mold on damp monsoon drains.

She picks up the sari and drapes the pallu coyly over a shoul-der. She looks at the ground and says, *This is the most beautiful thing I have ever owned.*

Sleep

The floor is red cement, cool
in Calcutta heat, the borders black
diamonds under bare feet.
A fierce grandfatherly snore
and the newsprint whirs
to the floor, stirred by a fan.
Up the steps, creeping past
the mezzanine. The women's room
reveals itself by a hushed giggle.

They are four on the ancient teak
bed in a disarray of muslin
petticoats, unhooked blouses,
and jasmine-scented hair spread
on white pillows, arranged as
a Tetris of female forms. Mashi
stirs slightly, pats the empty space
to cuddle into bare midriff.

My mother is not my mother;
she is happy.

The room paan-infused, opiates
stupefy the breeze. Chest curves
rising and falling. Buzz of flies,
the murmur of summer somnolence.

I pry open traitorous eyes again
and again, until a gentle rain
pitches me into dreams.

Dreamscapes: Haibun

Recurrent dreams take me back into a childhood home, to Wellington, New Zealand, through rooms I roamed between the ages of ten to fourteen. The sleep tracker tells me how restlessly I sleep; the purple REM bars tower over deep sleep, sometimes five in number, the log of rapid pulse and breath ranging in width and frequency, charting the frenzied territory of dreamscapes.

I awake midsentence, still speaking to people. Then realize that these are people I can only communicate with in dreams.

I send R a message. She is a remote Facebook friend now, to be remembered on birthdays and perhaps the New Year, although once we were inseparable. She still lives in the house next door, the house that shares a wide garden and outdoor shed with my childhood home, the dusty shed a wooden building into which we dragged a discarded mattress so we could spend nights there. We would creep out of back doors, swinging out of large bay windows, treading lightly on stairs lit by the moon.

R is surprised to hear from me. She thinks I heard her mother passed away some months ago.

I had no idea. Her mother, just a few hours ago, rolled out spicy lentil papads flavored with cumin seeds and asafetida, to be dried in the sun. She instructed me on how the edges must lie round and flat on the white muslin—*like this, exactly!*—and then refashioned mine with the rebellious, curling edge. She sat in the middle of Gujarati women whose fingers were chopping or kneading, others had thin wooden rolling pins—belans—in hand. This group laughed often and called each other behen—sister—even though they were, like me, unrelated by blood.

These dreams have recurred over days, until they feel more real than waking up in a cold Chicago, the sky as bleak as the news, an inbox filled with disappearing opportunities.

The dreams take me into a specific house, and the rooms and corridors within. They do not take me to the street corner where I smoked my first cigarette with friends, gasping as the acrid taste burned my throat. The dreams do not take me through the winding hills of my paper route around Newton, chased by a dog as I ran shrieking for shelter. They do not take me to the Gandhi Center of the weekly bharata natyam dance lessons, past the park where boys would lie in wait, pelting stones and shouting racial slurs.

These dreams take me straight into a home where the smells of cooking waft over the heads of the loud and busy women, a place as warm as the food.

I express my condolences to R. Then, hesitantly, I tell her about my dreams. R is curious, and not at all disbelieving. She feels her mother's presence everywhere.

R asks about my mother, who now lives a continent away from me.

Do you talk to your mother often? I remember how you would have these awful fights, then not speak to each other for days.

I am blindsided. My childhood memories are erased by adult filial piety. There was an expiry date on resentment when I became a parent; I clearly saw the process of child-rearing as a series of omissions and confusion, any success as serendipity.

R's words splinter my history. I resolve to call my mother.
While I still can.

Nothing lies deeper.

In dank soil wait buried seeds

of what had once bloomed.

Buddham Sharanam Gachchami

Amitabha is a common name.
In India, Nepal, cities through Southeast Asia, it signifies
boundless (mit as bound, amit the opposite); my brother is
Amitabha,
            Buddha, of Immeasurable Light and Life.
After my brother's accident, I rushed to my altar,
            lit sandalwood, switched on the light
of many buddhas carved into stone, holy and potent.

The electric bulb sputtered, then died.
Incensed at this betrayal, I plugged in a new bulb,
            then another,
            tearing apart packaging,
            wires, tiny screws,
            aligning frayed colors and metal
            and stars.
The light would not switch on.
    Twenty-fourth of January a bus hit my brother,
        still twenty-fourth in Chicago;
            twenty-four Buddha figures,
                resolute in darkness, six on four sides.

I had a flight to catch. Before that, a universe to bend.

The poet Iqbal said:
khudi ko kar buland itna   Make your will so unyielding
ke har taqdeer se pehle,   that God must ask
Khuda bande se khud pooche, bata,   at each fork of destiny,
teri raza kya hai?   What is your desire?

On a bedside lamp with a flat base, a laddered stem reaching
the light,
I glued the ox-bone Buddha from Bhutan,

carried to the altar my wrathful offering:
Here! Return Amit in any avatar,
a single precious Buddha in place
of Immeasurable Light and Life,
arraign his history unbroken,
on this ladder to light.

The light switched on.

A glow suffused the golden Buddha face,
benevolent Amitabha's right hand
in bhumisparshamudra, rooted to earth,
turning anger to wisdom,
the universe indulgent of human hubris.

My vegetative brother lives.
But who *wanted* this?

Awshukh: Disease

Awshukh in Bengali, my mother tongue,
is opposite (aw) of shukh (contentment);
being ill is Awsukh. Dis-ease seems
similar, but you don t catch Awshukh,
it catches you until ontologically
discontent, you are fevered, in bed.

Once in a coma, now vegetative,
my brother is a two-year-old dribbling drool,
communicating (at times) with thumb (*yes*),
forefinger (*no*), raising a middle finger
for rude emphasis. He is Awshukh, but Disease
spreads through the house. My mother screams
at nurses, the help, the scavenging monkeys.
She calls her children *Murderers*. Papa remembers
nothing. Another brother, holding the fort, managing
moods, medicines, neurosurgeons, acupressure,
says little until he explodes.

We know how martyrs die,
I see one in gestation.

A maternal aunt was mentally ill; she died
    beaten and alone. I feel Disease
coursing my blood,   Awshukh waiting
multiplying   malignant,
destroying   love,
all ease,
      snuffing   contentment.

Monsoon: Delhi

This house I have rented
is melancholic, lights
lopsided in an alcoholic
line of wobbly forms.
The door squeaks: *Nothing*
Nothing fits.

It is a house of men:
one lone, the other lonely.

The guard is a young migrant,
his voice a nightly lullaby
distilling pain into a mobile
as the wind shivers a damp breath
of reined-in rain.

I guess at words in the dark,
hear the sad music of sibilants,
and fear this city of violent needs.

This house is at a junction, positioned
at a poisoned Vastu. Crystal chimes
clinker in the yowling wind. Everywhere
the smells of feeding, feasting.

K Block, Chittaranjan Park

Once, Chittaranjan Park's summer nights were darkened

by sudden load-shedding, then lit up by the procession

of torches, candlelit neighbors pouring into the streets

like Diwali, a community gathering without feast

or festival; we slept under stars on rooftops and woke

to sunshine shadowed by crows, always crows,

harbingers of a new dawn; *Top of the Pops* on the radio

and *Chitrahaar* on TV, everyone gathered around the set

for the Sunday movie, Pujas beginning with a stereo of

sound from neighboring radios at dawn; sneaking into

movies, *Summer of '42*, wearing redder lips and blacker

kohl and tiptoeing on stilettos to be older; life as

a conversation on hilltops and water tanks, words taking us

the long way home, past the Gurdwara, the GK II M-Block

Market, past the cigarette seller who wouldn't sell

fags to girls, past Shiv Mandir and Kalkaji, just to keep

going; everything took time, shopping at Lajpat Nagar

was a slow cough of smoke-filled roads past Moolchand,

our dupatta masks against pollution and preying men;

we had stomachs of steel and tongues on fire, ate

phuchkas at Market No 1 licking last bits of the tamarind

chili and potato and asking for more *tikha, aur tikha*;

conches heralded the sunset, temple bells chimed an

arati over rooftops and the woodsmoke-scented air of

winter; over badminton courts where my brothers

and I squabbled, sat draping shawls tighter, holding

friends closer, sipping chai in that elastic uncomplicated

time, steeped in the promise of immortality.

Going back to where I'm from

is to return to women who are goddesses,
incense smoke, and drumbeats & women
who bury infant girls in the ground, into
milk vats to drink until they drown;

to many-armed goddesses who slay
demons, and darkness, and scarcity
of thought & women who are womb
and vagina, never brain or mouth;

to stargazers who send probes to Mars,
mathematicians of cosmic poetry & women
raped in temples, strung from trees,
disemboweled in a dark-tinted moving bus;

to Bengal and Indus Valley and Chittaranjan Park
& Texas and Ohio and State Street in Chicago;

to meals beginning with bitter gourd and ending
in milky sweets & sweet-water fish, and mountain
goat, and homemade cheese strained through muslin
so fine it passes through a child's golden ring.

The mind travels as a flume,
belonging here, rooting nowhere;

the hunger for roads packed with parched
red earth; July, the monsoon cool of runny
streets, clouds paused for the miracle
of light on water, the sky's tandav;

rains feel amniotic as the nomad
breaststrokes through alien streets
for electric air, even as a belligerent

hunger pushes the boat away from shore;

I am more than a dress or a sari,
more than henna and bindi & more
than skin scabbed with regrowth.

                              Still so far to travel,
                                 higher to climb,
                              so much to uncage.

Two teenage girls were gang-raped and then hanged from a tree in a village in the northern state of Uttar Pradesh.

—Reuters, May 29, 2014

Turn away

from hemp ropes on slender necks, the embroidery glinting on a kameez, let susurrations visit the unrooted. Was the younger almost asleep, tunelessly humming, when the older hissed, *Come, I need to go now*, water can in hand toward malignant fields? The villagers squat on dusty haunches, think of moonglint on unfastened buckles, khaki pants, the thrust of earth rising. There is anger, and lewd spectacle, in the gaze of old men.

Sing, sing the myths of Mother Earth unzipped as refuge. Oh, Mithya—Lies!—look, babies unshoveled into the earth blossom only into meat, swinging from the sky.

This Shawl

*The hideous gang-rape in Delhi is part of the continuum of violence
millions of Indian women face every single day.*

—The Hindu, December 19, 2012

In Delhi, drape age as a shawl. Be silent. Invisible.
The decades shield a body, the spreading contours (like
a burqa in the wind) merely hinting at sexuality.
   Sometimes
—not always—age allows freedom to pass through piss-
filled back lanes, untouched by men who catcall and jostle
against breasts, masturbate on buses, reach out to fondle
a pubis publicly.

Years ago, a broken bus in Delhi forced a night walk
past the ramparts of Purana Qila. Dimly lit turns
towered, each shapechanger Rape in its mustachioed
menace, destroying the only thing a young woman is
responsible for safeguarding: her impenetrability.
Her mate, her education, the dominion of others.

Through the years this shawl, stained by the slow drip
of semen on a local train, the sudden shock of a penis
behind the guise of a lost traveler near home, the embrace
of a male relative, a stranger's grope; this shawl, woven
with the collective memories of women shamed by
Why only you? How did you ask for it; this shawl, like
our dupattas and anchals, meagre veils against men
brought up badly; this shawl knows how tenuous
the threads, how easily torn . . . this shawl,
is now part of the communal sloughing,
slouching uneasily toward losing
all our cover-ups.

Rewound

You were not like the boys who would sneak into class
and leave notes on my desk (smeared chutney and ink),
you were not into bold nor too shy deference,
no wild words, like heartbeats, marched wanton in lines.

I could well comprehend as the foreign-returned
how I reigned with large breasts bred on clean wholesome air
Delhi's smog had not marked me, nor Indian sun,
(though my glowing complexion would brown in six months).
As a veteran of crushes, I already knew
of the heartbreak—and titillation—of the dark side.

I could not bewitch you, not even a sly glance,
when in passing I'd slow in pretend nonchalance—
again pass that canteen, stop and go, one more time—
you were fearless with food, dangerous in your fame,
never asked me for notes never whispered at all:
Did you finish that test? Sometime, I . . . can I call?

When we finally held clammy hands in the dark
of the cinema hall still too bright for our needs,
between closed-mouthed kisses your hand wandered, then
stopped, abashed. When I had to return to my home
I could die but you said you would love only me
forever. It took two months to find someone new.

I would hear after years you had been in a jail
(drunk driving? accident? it was too long ago)
I would hear that you were still too *different* . . . alone . . .
and I'd feel the dark hall, a still wandering hand,
new magic, and the sizzle of endless possibility.

After the Ice Storm

The tree beyond my kitchen window bends in ice
tight glassiness in its low droop
limbs touching the ground in long talons

the frost has it shrouded in white.
But a few rebel spikes
burst through the damp snow, and this tree

after three decades gives me my grandmother.
And I am a child again
held between tight bony knees

squirming on slick steps
while she kneads my scalp with coconut oil
mixed with the essence of hibiscus.

She has my slithering body tight in her grasp
as she bends over
a quasimodic hunch bearing many burdens

while her hair rebels from her own shaved head
it bursts into spikes
from a lushness within.

She says, *Hair grows lustrous on a beautiful woman.*
A man, encircled in its silky cloud,
never wants to leave.

I touch the icicles of a frosty winter,
feeling her benediction
in the prickle of my scalp.

A Question

When the air frizzes with thoughts squirming like catfish
    battered to death, on such a day, my father looks over
    the newspaper (he is so shrunken, so much smaller)
    and peers into my raging eyes—
—*Ma? Why do we think we are exempt from disaster? That bad*
    things that happen, cannot happen to us?

My father—at 94—has lost his parents, and all seven
    siblings:

He is the last one still alive to remember the color of
    eight types of village spinach, the slime of river mud
    in his toes, the taste of sweet-river fish captured in
    handwoven baskets;

He remembers days of a full home, unsevered
    communities—an unpartitioned homeland;

He remade himself in a rifle factory, a homeopathic clinic,
    many diplomatic enclaves. His avatars speak fluent
    anomie.
—*What is it that makes us so special, to be exempt from life?*

I take my father's gnarled hand,
                each skein sprouting a story.
        His fingers zigzag through newsprint
              past caravans of walking migrants
                     the chimera of home.

These Words Once Danced in Red Jooties

These words would once burst through that door
in flaming silk, rustling aquamarine

they would raise one hand, thick with silver tinkling
swish the air and tilt the chin

to demand attention. These words once knew
the power of insouciance.

These words once danced in red jooties
sliding a foot, slyly, just like a tongue;

kissed the floor, skirts trailing low on swinging hips.
These words drenched themselves in color

nipples like seeds through thin white fabric
they rampaged through streets, breath sour with bhang.

These words could, would sometimes, be bashful.
Not often—but often enough—to conceal

the coquette with many lovers. They sprinted; they twirled;
they climbed; they soared. This has brought them far.

Now these words sit in oak-paneled rooms with snow outside.
One button fastened on the herringbone jacket

black nylon itching below an A-line skirt. They stress
initial consonants, schwa vowels, lose aspirations, sift
morphemic phonemic nonsense into essence,
pause to measure syntax, weigh pragmatics.

A tongue protrudes in anxious anticipation
of spilling instead of blending.

Printers Row, Chicago

I come to Chicago
resisting assimilation.

From old cities in Europe
to the older ruins of Asia,
I have resisted the hyphenations,
the identity reconstructions,
of tired-huddled masses,
in this adulterated corner
of the globe.

Until, in Printers Row
—in an antiquarian bookshop,
red-bricked from 1896—
a man reads from the distressed
first edition of the *Rime*, hardcover
separated from spine, stark lines drawn
above an idle ship on a painted ocean.
He knows Tagore, and on his desktop
is the image of Waheeda,
incandescent beauty.

He talks about translators,
epics, New York broadsides.
In that tiny shop, lays bare the
nuance—the proclivity of
imagination—this audacious new world.

While his guitar gently weeps, I turn

to State, past Lake, follow the melody drizzling
melancholy into a Chicago night, lake breeze
a caress of yearning, for *yesterday, yay yay.*
I am drawn to this: a busker, his stage the street,
strumming a guitar, his voice soaring over
the traffic hum as he begins, *Here comes the sun.*
I lean against Walgreens, with a homeless mother
and child. Rowdy teens cross over, hurtling
hooded—they circle and zoom, surround him—
shouting *Beat It!* He smiles and complies.
Jackson's "Beat It" wickedly segues
to Weird Al and the boys shout *Eat it!*
the music unceasing on this easy
congregation of grace. The evening news
scrolls on the ABC marquee "Death toll . . ."
but we dance, singing with mingling exultant
breath, over this transient field of joy.

At Door County, Wisconsin

Breathe in. Pine
and birch,   red oak
branches stroke
    air, striped
garter
    snake
        startles
to slither.
    Queen
Anne's lace
    quivers
impossible symmetry.
    Coupled dragonflies
        soar to
    roar of water,
smooth
    jagged
        rock, purple
lake
slaking
ball
of fire.
        Butterflies swoop,
swing;   crinkling
bumblebees in
    tinkling air.
        Geese ink
    flight through
flaming sky.

Shhhh,
whisper waves . . .

                    shanti
                    shanti,
                    shanti.

Dynamite

The bus takes the curve
on Wacker Drive,
past the Tribune Tower,
past the new Apple store.
A boy, perhaps eight,
whips out his phone,
shouts, *Look! It's THAT Tower!*
He takes a photo,
carefully
fitting T, the final M and P
in the phone frame,
click-clicks,
turns to siblings to ask,
Anyone got some dynamite?
This is Chicago,
so we smile.
This golden boy
with his family
(father, mother,
two siblings)
on holiday,
freckled and free,
with eyes as blue
as the Chicago River.

Descent from the Winter Garden

Behind me on the escalator is a young man, perhaps
   twenty,
at least a foot taller. We are alone in this narrow corridor
   going down,
leaving the light of the Winter Garden, the library hushed
   in this space with no one
else but us. He steps down and my neck feels this move,
   cranes to read the walls, strains
so that I am looking up and behind— "If it had been
   possible
to build the Tower of Babel without ascending it, the work
would have been permitted—FRANZ KAFKA"—my brows
   furrowed
to construct meaning from disappearing ink on grey walls.
He lopes down three more steps,
and I bound off the escalator,
my heart a-pounding,
unreasonable thing,
powering my feet.

After the rallies for I Can't Breathe,
Hands Up, Don't Shoot,
at the gathering
of fierce voices
for the political,
a poet brought
marbled paper
to scratch words
with spent bullets;
I etched "My memory
is again in the way
of your history—

AGHA SHAHID ALI"
as lush calligraphy,
colored in red,
white, and blue.

Now, all alone,
color is merely perilous,
a phenotype.

Dreamers, 2017

2017 has been that year.
Now doors zap a shock at entry,
handles sting ferocious, forcing
supplication. Feel your way through
walls and frames to lessen the charge.
Even chargers jolt unwary
hands, clothes fit snugly but peel off
in prickly betrayal, sizzling
hair maliciously. Messages
patronize—trying to help—codes
to quiet down, or leave. Don't
speak of past seasons of mellow
fruitfulness, don't walk through black ice,
the impatient gales are growling:
The Dream is so pale, too pale,
beyond what you may imagine.

Foreign Passport

When they took my nine-year-old son
to a barricaded place
the noise of O'Hare Airport
was drowned by the rushing of my blood.

His passport was too foreign.

They said, *There is a lookout,*
the computers are slow, it may take some time.
I could see my nine-year-old son blinking
as they led him away.

I was not to be silenced.

The officer marched out,
      unfurled venom from tight lips,
            and hissed: *Do you know*
                 how many people were killed
                    in the Twin Towers?
                  I saw vultures
             circling the fields of the dead
        shadows on the Euphrates
    but I said, *What do you think*
my son had to do with it?

She spun on her heels, saying,
You are a guest in this country.
End of conversation.

It was four long hours.

Say the Names

My name is Simran.
I am Sikh.

> *Thousands of dollars in donations*
> *will soon be heading to the victims*
> *of the Sikh temple shooting in Wisconsin.*
> *A check was presented to*
> *Fresno Police Chief Jerry Dyer*
> *for the officer shot outside the temple.*

When we die,
don't we still
have names?

> *Wade Michael Page, 40,*
> *died of a gunshot wound*
> *after he killed six worshippers,*
> *wounded three others*
> *as they prepared for Sunday services*
> *at the Sikh Temple of Wisconsin*
> *in Oak Creek on August 5.*

My mother makes
spinach with onion-garlic-
cumin, adding a dash of
secret masala; she slathers
it on a tortilla with
a pat of butter.
She sprays the house
after she cooks,
until it reeks of Febreze
and ocean breeze,
lavender dreams distilled

40

in bedrooms; she wants the
house to smell *Amreekan.*

> *The fatal shooting happened on Sunday*
> *at the Sikh Temple of Wisconsin,*
> *where six people were killed*
> *and another three badly injured.*
> *The gunman, named*
> *Wade Michael Page,*
> *was then shot by an officer.*

At school
I eat pizzas;
my friends
call me Sam.

> *Brian Murphy, 51,*
> *shot Sunday, is now recovering*
> *after a second surgery,*
> *Oak Creek Police Chief*
> *John Edwards said.*

In red-yellow-blue-orange
turbans and gauzy scarves,
we mourn black and white,
holding up photographs,
lighting names with candles.

> We are   invisible   in death.

> *Six people killed in Sikh place of worship*
> The tragedy finds half-rhymes
> *Stamp out the hate, ramp up the love*
> but no one dirges the names

Paramjit Kaur,
Sita Singh,
Ranjit Singh,
Satwant Singh Kaleka,
Prakash Singh,
Suveg Singh Khattra

When the Granthi
leads a hymn in Punjabi,
I want him to toll names
like church bells:

PARAMJIT KAUR,
SITA SINGH,
RANJIT SINGH,
SATWANT SINGH KALEKA,
PRAKASH SINGH,
SUVEG SINGH KHATTRA

I know naming won't bring them back.

The house
smells of ocean breeze and lavender,
the frozen spinach uncooked,
no traces of masala.
I wait
for my mother
to speak again.

Death: A Crow

A crow swoops in,
picks at my lunch plate
then sits on the rafters and eyes me.

I imagine bugs and dung with crow breath,
deliberate on whether to bin my food,
or offer it whole to the crow, like we did,
when my father-in-law passed away.
The rituals in Malaysia are diasporic,
any change measured as loss, guarded
fiercely by matriarchs unlettered
in the Vedas they staunchly defend.

It was an excess of offerings, of dishes
loved by the deceased, Chinese Mun Fun
from Fusion, fish and chips from The Ship,
red wine and omum water. Nothing
loved in life left out in death.

Women woke at four to cook,
producing kochur saag,
koi macher jhal, labra,
mushuri dal, mutton, fish
of four kinds, shops scoured
from Brickfields to Taman Tun
for the vines of the pumpkin.
The widow insisted on more,
yet another dish to be fried
and curried, any feast too meager
to satiate the loss of a companion
of sixty years.

If a crow feeds on the food
it is the return of the soul.
Don't look back at the riverbank.
Let the departed feast once more
on earthly morsels, in any form.

                    I, the rebel, wanted no part of this,
                no ritualism made possible by the labor
                    of tired women to feed mere animals.
                    I had work to do, lawyers to see.

Mourners returned to food piled
on trestle tables, ate under the weight
of a gourmand no longer there; so much
food destined for waste, as much of life is,
bones and flesh to river silt.

                Now, two days after my father-in-law's ashes
                    are immersed in Benares, countries away
                    from where he took a last breath, a crow
                sits silently tasting my food, daring me to eat.
        And I eat it all, every last morsel, going back for seconds;
                this delicious meal of dal with sajna, potato-peas
                    with rice, which Daddy would have relished.

I do not offer the crow my tasted food but he watches
while I eat,
        then flies up
                    and away
                            on the applause
                                    of wings.

Supermoon in April

I am the beginning, the staying, and the end of creation; I am the womb and the eternal seed.

—Bhagavad Gita

Like water poured
into a vessel—in
the dark—gurgles
to signal fullness,
my father says, I'm dying,
then, in an alien tongue,
whispers, "Wait, wait, wait . . ."

And I fly through the night
over land wan with snow,
afloat with a supermoon.
This Herb Moss Pink Moon,
Sprouting Grass Moon,
Paschal Moon, this Fish Moon
glows over Greenland, blazes
over Ittoqqortoormiit as I
plead, "Wait, wait, wait . . ."

And he does. When he passes
in days, there is his shell
to cremate, mantras to invoke
three generations, the named
calling out to name-givers.
My father gave me
Dipika, resplendent
beams of a gentle moon.
Clear-eyed by what I carry,
unblinded by glare, I see

an orb constant, sighted
from far away, waning,
waxing. Always, waiting.

Learning Not to Apologize

In a clinic in Kuala Lumpur, a nurse wiped my tears;
I was unable to move. He asked, *Do you want this?*
I didn't call my mother; it was my secret for too long,
until it wouldn't contain itself, words like the seepage
of blood resolute on release. Until the night I told
my sons a story, my boys uncomprehending warm
weights in my arms, the night abuzz with tropical
fecundity, a jasmine susurration in the breeze
perfuming the vastness where nothing is still,
nothing unchanging, nothing ever truly gone.

Saudade

the voluptuousness of misery

—Machado de Assis

In Itaparica, the beach broods
under cruddy sky, two fishermen
and I search waves spitting
shells: ribbed green, a crown
for a queen; a conch; an obelisk;
a whorled shell; a thin, swell
pink modicum of a disc.

I wash the five in running water.
The pink slithers through fingers—
fragmented it lingers . . .

                               disappears.

A wound reappears
periodically swelling,
voluptuous
            with reproach.

Benign Negligence

My parenting style is benign
negligence; plotting books,
poetry, busy at the stove,
half-listening to talk
of soccer goals or how
the senate council will
make money this year.
I know too well those
other times—when home
is the only place to melt
from cool, the tantrums,
the door-slams—
yearning to be free.

Then, he leaves. I remember
light in his eyes when words
tripped almost incoherent.
I see in the child the man
he is becoming; I see him
so rarely now. That toddler
who stretched out expansive
arms all the way back
to show how much he loved
now uses that gesture on video
to silently say, *I miss you.*

Childbirth doesn't prepare
you for this. I am an owl
touched by the light—
yearning for the moon.

Migration, Exile . . . These Are Men's Words

Migration, exile . . . these are men's words.
Women have always been torn up
like rice seedlings to be replanted
in marriage (or another name);
my language weeps its wedding melodies
in many dialects, many tunes—
In my next life, O God, don't make me a daughter—

Exile, Migration. . . what meaning then?

I am no woman-poet-migrant-in-exile.
Keep your labels, please.

I am not tamed by toil, shoulders stiff
with xenophobia, nor a person of color
shunted to workshops where grievances
grow in collegiality. I am a nomad,
homeless, rootless, I am the zephyr—
the vayu that breezes past rooted trees—
I swish past suburbs, four-bedroomed homes,
theatered basements, the two-car garage;
nothing stops me as I skim by brooks,
snake to large rivers, course by course,
I am fed by a hunger, sharper than
life, to live in this; to suck bare
a skin, tender as peeled lychees, always
terrified that there may not be another
rebirth to appeal to.

I find my muse as much as she finds
me, without home or temple, veena
in hand, book in another,
in the feminine infinite
we make our home.

The Dialect of Distant Harbors

Bengali is my father tongue. It's true my mother speaks
Bengali and crooned *Phule phule dhole dhole*
over sleepy infant heads, but it was my father
who grounded Bengali, watered curlicues of text,
weeded enunciation through teenage years
when English whispered, *Put your head on my shoulder.*
When Indian schools spat out Vernacular,
as the dark peasant destined for penury, English
strutted like a boss. But my father recited Tagore,
the Bengali sibilants a song on his tongue,
Bohu din dhore, bohu krosh dure:
I have traveled miles, spent years afar,
seen mountains and oceans new,
but I haven't seen, outside my door,
paddy glinting in morning dew.

Bengali is the *seventh* most spoken language of our world.

It will not disappear by my neglect, nor Bengali poets
    writing in English.
It is impervious to our mad dashes and enjambments, our
    stutters in severed
tongues. Yet I fear the absences from the vocabulary of my
    children—
Seventh most spoken language of the world, but its majesty
    unfelt
in this foreign tongue I continue to write in, to reach you . . .
        . . . to reach you.

Bengali is still my magic chalice
refilled by the dialect of distant harbors.

A Diptych at the Seaside

1.

She collects seashells, three
in a row. One domed, a Buddhist
stupa; another, sleek, hugs
the ground, an earthworm
after spring rain, seeking damp
new earth to nuzzle; the third
is halved, amputated, an orange
tongue searching for its mate.

A shell on land is life
made nomad, seeking home.

She wants to live again
in that house on stilts, taste
the sharpness of anchovies
dried on bamboo vines.

2

His pursuit of her, once,
had thrummed like sleeplessness
within the covers of a great book.

He is a purveyor of words,
chipping at monuments, stupas
of the ancients in his brain. Her
needs, the small talk, tire him
he is afraid of hours wasted,
knowledge of giants undecoded.

A memory of wild hair,
evenings satiny and humid.

She comes from a land
where women stand over rice pots
incanting the moon.

He looks at her crouched,
collecting seashells, and sees.
The bend of her neck lifting,
marking the way home.

Keeping the Faith

Mcleodganj is hallowed, the Dalai Lama's
home in exile. Spirits of British soldiers
roam bare churches while the Himalayan wind
drizzles bereavement.

Death in exile. Terrible certainties dog
Tibet's faithful fleeing to India, leaving
family, home, and language for Dharamshala:
Home of the faithful.

Temple bells chime in McLeodganj as prayers
float heavenward, spun by hands praying for lost
lands, His Holiness. Mandalas center hope,
faith is lit by lamps.

Bulbuls call, kites ride the breeze. Nothing festive
sounds merrily in this place of acute loss.
Momo sellers, wrapping snacks at the bazaar,
speak of dead children.

Cyclical eternal knots. Though boots and guns
circumnavigate Potala with pilgrims,
people dream of holy lakes with ancestors
merging with the fish.

Hindustani Musalman: An Indian Muslim

by Hussain Haidry
Translated from Hindi/Urdu with Udit Mehrotra

On an evening stroll down my street,
the azan echoes, stops my feet,
reminds me it is time to pray,
but I start musing on that day:

Bhai, what kind of Muslim am I?

Am I Shia or am I Sunni?
Am I Khoja or am I Bohri?
From the village or the city?
Am I a rebel or a mystic?
Am I devout or sophistic?

Bhai, what kind of Muslim am I?

Do I prostrate in submission
or am headed to perdition?
Is my cap my identity,
or the beard shaved off completely?

Recite Quranic verse, I could,
or hum the songs of Bollywood?
Do I chant *Allah* every day,
or fight the Sheiks in every way?

What kind of Muslim am I, bhai?
I know I'm an Indian Muslim.

I'm from the Deccan, and UP,
I'm from Bhopal, and from Delhi,
I'm Gujarati, and Bengali,

I'm from the high castes and lower,
I'm the weaver and the cobbler,
I'm the doctor and the tailor.

The holy Gita speaks in me,
an Urdu newsprint thrives in me,
divine is Ramadan in me,
the Ganges washes sins in me.
I live by my rules, not for you,
I've smoked a cigarette or two.
No politician rules my veins,
no party has me in their chains,

for I am an Indian Muslim.

I'm in Old Delhi's Bloody Gate,
I'm in Lucknow's magical maze,
I'm in Babri's demolished dome,
I'm in the blurred borders of home,
in the poverty of slum dwellings,
the madrasa's shattered ceilings,
the embers flaming a riot,
I'm in the garment stained with blood

I'm Hindustani Musalman.

The Hindu temple door is mine,
as are the mosque minarets mine,
the Sikh gurdwara hall is mine,
the pews in churches also mine;
I am fourteen in one hundred,
but in these fourteen not othered,
I am within all of hundred,
and hundred is the sum of me.

Don't view me any differently,

I have a hundred ways to be
my hundred nuanced characters,
from hundreds of storytellers.

Brother, as Muslim as I am,
I'm that much also Indian.

I'm Hindustani Musalman,
                    I'm Hindustani Musalman.

Sempiternal Fire

For M. F. Husain (1915–2011)

At ninety-five, these hands are still in thrall;
a curve of hip, the lash of eye, the flash
of breast, a dancer's back—all rise and fall.

A symphony still spirals through my brush.
I sweep the canvas colored, I rewrite
the censorship of fools, the righteous blush

at nudity of gods. Alas, my flight
to exile is not imaginary;
like childhood scribbles on mud floors, lamplit,

my shadow-hand looms giant and wary
over my creations. Will my art last?
I most fear death, as they will not bury

my body with kin, but far from my past,
far from the Mumbai that speaks my tongue, rife
with movie billboards— a curvaceous cast

all cleavage and lips—much larger than life—
in wet white saris unwrappable girls;
the money pours in. But gods, like a wife,

must be fully-clad, wholesome, not unfurl.
I, barefoot Muslim at temples ancient,
am too pagan, bold, in this dizzy hurl

toward a modern Hindutva. No scent
of nuance, so I paint cinematic
large, brash, this Holy Trinity: Present

Destroyer first, not last. Shiv kinetic
with snakes and floods, rich in matted icons
to execute. Preserver, lethargic

Vishnu, androgynous, taking no stance,
in blind complicit middle. Last, Creator
Brahma pared to third-eye-one-head essence . . .

flame leaping from mind to hand to acquire
a legacy, of sempiternal fire.

Amsterdam!

Amsterdam, you will never be my city.
Graffiti sprayed on demolished doors:
"Please forgive me father
for I am ready to sin"—
and the purple latex pants
on phallic road hedgers—
so much perv-art,
ponderous posturing.

Off the Dam Square
blue-lit bodies pose on sale
as the tour group goose-steps,
hoisting yellow parasols
under a pissing sky;
just there, a body
is scraped off the pavement
like mashed patat with mayonnaise.

One detests canals after the eighty-eighth.
I yearn for spice in my tea,
for heated conversations,
for sunsets smelling of cow dung and incense.
And yet—

the day before Koninginnedag
when the boy drew a careful square
labeling it *bezet*,
the old woman grumbled about Nazi words,
picked up his broken chalk,
and squatted by the road
painting small wooden squares tulip-red,
a crimson barrier for the flowering plants.

Everyone's a Rembrandt here.
The city belongs to no one
yet everyone's its curator.

Guan Yin in the Huangshan

The Yellow Mountains tower and swoop like eagles
with ragged rocks like stalagmite claws,
and feathery pine trees.
In the North Sea area a tall rock pierces the sky
like a caped woman with a lotus in her hand;
it's the Guan Yin Peak.

The pilgrims all stop here.

Lovers lock locks, then throw away keys,
red ribbons of wishes flutter in the breeze.
But it is only a rock to my eye, maybe shaped
like a woman but not so unlike others
springing from the mountains, so many
could be slim goddesses. Then the guide says,
closing his eyes, *One can see her only HERE*—
he strikes a fist on his heart.

In the Huangshan Mountains, a photo is taken
of a blood-red sky torn birthing the sun,
—from Brightness Top, the peaks are shadowed black—
but one, the Guan Yin Peak, stands haloed round the head
centering the light, unmistakably woman-figured,
lotus in her hand.

Sometimes the third eye is a camera,
sometimes a fist to the heart.

Mountain Echoes

In Bhutan, the mountains call with peals
of prayer bells, mantras churned by brooks
as pilgrims trek a weary path
to the Taktsang Dzong, where a holy man
soared to heavenly heights
on the back of his woman tiger.
Legends spring from rocks here
of the eternal through ambrosial waters.
The Buddha looms large in bhumisparshamudra,
touching earth, rooted here.

Yellow tsatsas, in the red shade of spinning wheels
mingle cremated ashes into dusty clay.
Flags flutter a rainbow salvation,
as two little girls, like kittens in the sun,
settle next to me, on the wide rock.
The older speaks haltingly, the younger not at all
yet we play scissors-paper-stone
they teach me Dzongkha, gymtse-dho-shoko
grabbing hands to cut, cover, and swallow whole,
it's a language of flashing fingers,
palms turning black-and-white, naap-ya-karp
human babble jostling in amity.

I want them to win.
To always reach out
with such grace, such openness,
to gesture of crows-spider-horses,
to encapsulate a living world
in such mellifluous hands
within tiny folded palms.

Their laughter peals like the prayer bell
over these sheer cliffs, kissed by moist clouds
drenched in holy waters.

It May Have Been the Third Glass of Wine

The bowls set aside, surfeit with food, you opened the book,
spine peeling into meshed gauze of a College Street bookstall,
yellow-stickered invitations to multiple pages,
and you read on (the Bengali syllables singing in your throat
like the wine in my mouth). The room hushed
to the sound of your voice, like a primordial call
muffled by age, desolate
with unrequited love.

I remembered a young man from my girlhood,
fingers poised over a harmonium singing poetry;
later, in a dark theater, by the light of copulating
serpents, the young man had declared a mad
passion, but in his voice I only heard
words like incense, divine offerings.

Poets, I have loved, but it is never the man.
Nor the magic hour, nor even the words so fraught
with weight the tongue trips to contain them—
it's that sibilant *leap* ... yes,

Vayu and Agni,
breath on fire
combusting into flight.

Damp Red Earth and Pouring Rain (Pankti)

Writing a novel is a lot
like cooking a good biryani.
First the manic frying, the heat
of cardamom, cinnamon, cloves
bay leaves, star anise, peppercorns.

Then set aside. Revise. Onions
reborn caramelized, pungent
with ginger-garlic. A fragrant,
even, browning, then the meat thrown
into an osmotic simmer.

The basmati rice must be—just—
half cooked, mingling warm milk infused
with saffron and the essence of
pandan, sprinkled rosewater.
Then a final rearrangement.

Gently stir this meat-rice, layered
yet touching. Out with the spices
hard, embittered, harsh on the tongue.
Seal to steam—slowly—in its own
broth, then taste for imperfections.

It is merely meat and rice—yes—
but what you now hold in your hands
will transport you to open fields
of saffron blowing in the wind,
of damp red earth and pouring rain.

Aphorisms from the Malay Archipelago

In the fifth decade of life mothers are grandmothers,
matriarch of clans. Men unshackle, like hermits
seeking caves, detach to higher calling.

As quietly as the sweet potato burgeons, so quietly
does the iron rust. I, of east-west, modern-ancient,
wanted to glide

like flying squirrels, from areca to date frond,
certain I, not the wind, caused trees to sway.
Moored now, a pea

expelled from shell with no husk to shelter
under—what is gravy if it doesn't fall on
rice?—even the sunbird touches ground

or is an aphorism, a cautionary tale: no matter how
you chop water, it doesn't break. But uncontained,
what is water, but murky clay,

evanescent cloud diminished
to vapor?

Notes

"Buddham Sharanam Gachchami"
The poem includes a stanza from the poem "Khudi Ko Kar Buland Itna (Make Your Will So Unyielding)" by Allama Iqbal. Translation by Dipika Mukherjee.

"Turn away"
The epigraph comes from the following article: Bhalla, Nita. "Indian Teen Girls Gang-Raped and Hanged from a Tree—Police." Reuters, May 29, 2014. https://www.reuters.com/article/uk-india-killings/indian-teen-girls-gang-raped-and-hanged-from-a-tree-police-idUKKB-N0E91B220140529

"This Shawl"
The epigraph comes from the following editorial: "Time to Be Ashamed." Editorial. *The Hindu*, December 19, 2012. https://www.thehindu.com/opinion/editorial/time-to-be-ashamed/article4214334.ece

"The Dialect of Distant Harbors"
Phule phule dhole dhole is from a song by Rabindranath Tagore (1861–1941), a Bengali poet, novelist, musician, painter, playwright, and Nobel Laureate.

Tagore was influenced by Robert Burns's "Ye Banks and Braes," and this song takes a lilting tune to describe the birds and flowers of gardens in Bengal.

https://www.donovancrow.com/
the-banks-o-doon-e-banks-and-braes-robert-burns/

The poem is "Ekti Shishir Bindu (A Glistening Drop of Dew)" by Rabindranath Tagore. Translation by Dipika Mukherjee.

"Sempiternal Fire"
At the time of M. F. Husain's death at the age of ninety-six, eight large triptychs from the Indian Civilization series, the last works of this modern master, were completed. Husain died in exile and is buried outside London.

Amsterdam!
Koninginnedag, or Queen's Day, is a carnival-like event at the end of April each year in Amsterdam. It is a day-and-night party across the whole city with open markets in the streets.

"Damp Red Earth and Pouring Rain (Pankti)"
Pankti (associated with food and the god of rain) is a Vedic meter found in one of the later books (Book V) of the Rig Vida. The pankti meter is stanzaic with 40 syllables, written in any number of quintains, five padas, or feet of eight syllables.

Acknowledgments

Grateful acknowledgment to the editors of the journals, magazines, and anthologies where many of these poems first appeared, often in different form:

The Aerogram: "Death: A Crow," "Turn away"
Authors Electric: "At Door County, Wisconsin"
Chicago Quarterly Review: "Benign Negligence," "Damp Red Earth and Pouring Rain (Pankti)," "Descent from the Winter Garden," "Going back to where I'm from"
The Common: "Saudade"
Dimsum: "After the Ice Storm," "These Words Once Danced in Red Jooties"
Earthen Lamp Journal: "Printers Row, Chicago"
Fractured Literary: "A Diptych by the Seaside"
Freefall: "It May Have Been the Third Glass of Wine"
Life and Legends: "The Dialect of Distant Harbors," "Sempiternal Fire"
LossLit Magazine: "Awshukh: Disease"
The Mekong Review: "Aphorisms from the Malay Archipelago," "Keeping the Faith," "Monsoon, Delhi," "Sleep"
Mobius: The Journal of Social Change: "Dreamers"
New Writing Dundee 4: "Amsterdam!"
Newcity: "Dynamite," "Supermoon in April," "While his guitar gently weeps, I turn"
Pandemic Publications: "Dreamscapes"
Poetry Quarterly: "Mountain Echoes"

Poetry@Sangam: "Migration, Exile . . . These Are Men's
    Words," "Rewound," "Turn away"
Quiddity: "K Block, Chittaranjan Park"
RHINO: "Wanderlust Ghazal"
United Verses: An Anthology: "Guan Yin in the Huangshan"
Vestal Review: "Bangkok, 1959"
World Literature Today: "Hindustani Musalman: An Indian
    Muslim," "Say the Names"

"After the Ice Storm," "Amsterdam!" "Foreign Passport,"
"Guan Yin in the Huangshan," "It May Have Been the
Third Glass of Wine," "Migration, Exile . . . These Are Men's
Words," "Mountain Echoes," "Printers Row, Chicago," "Re-
wound," "Say the Names," "These Words Once Danced in
Red Jooties," "This Shawl," and "Turn away" appeared in The
Third Glass of Wine published by Writers Workshop India,
2015, and are reprinted with permission.

"After the Ice Storm," "Foreign Passport," "It May Have
Been the Third Glass of Wine," and "These Words Once
Danced in Red Jooties" also appeared in The Palimpsest of
Exile published by Rubicon Press, 2009.

Deepest gratitude to Write On, Door County, and Jerod
Santek, for graciously offering a residency in Wisconsin
in September 2021, during which I was able to polish and
finish this manuscript.

I am grateful for my Chicago writing group, and their
patience through rounds of editing—Toni, Vivek, Nina,
Sushma, Ravi, Faisal—thank you.

My gratitude to the CavanKerry team—Joan, Gabe, Baron,
Joy, Ryan, Dimitri, Dana, Tamara, and Elena—for honoring
my words in the best possible way and for creating a space
for writing that opens up the world.

80

My family has been my greatest source of inspiration and my unflagging cheerleaders. The Mukherjees in Delhi (Pratima, Ashis, Ishita, and Sreoshi) fill my poetry and feed my soul. To the Dutts in the US (Prasanta, Arohan, and Arush), thank you for putting up with my absences even when I am physically present. Deepest gratitude to Arohan for being my best beta reader, always. This book is for my father; Papa, thank you for the gift of a magic chalice, filled with the dialect of distant harbors.

CavanKerry's Mission

A not-for-profit literary press serving art and community, CavanKerry is committed to expanding the reach of poetry and other fine literature to a general readership by publishing works that explore the emotional and psychological landscapes of everyday life, and to bringing that art to the underserved where they live, work, and receive services.

Other Books in the Notable Voices Series

BEAR, Karen Chase
Fun Being Me, Jack Wiler
Common Life, Robert Cording
The Origins of Tragedy & Other Poems, Kenneth Rosen
Apparition Hill, Mary Ruefle
Against Consolation, Robert Cording

This book was printed on paper from responsible sources.

Dialect of Distant Harbors has been set in Joanna Nova, an update to Eric Gill's original Joanna typefaces from 2001. It was designed by Ben Jones of Monotype Studio in 2015.